W9-BHX-995

You're a Gent, Andy Capp!

by
Smythe

A FAWCETT GOLD MEDAL BOOK

Fawcett Books, Greenwich, Connecticut

YOU'RE A GENT, ANDY CAPP!

ANDY CAPP of the Daily Mirror, London

© 1974, 1975 IPC Newspaper Ltd.

© 1978 CBS Publications, The Consumer Publishing
Division of CBS Inc.

All rights reserved

Copyright under International and Pan-American Copyright
Conventions.

A Fawcett Gold Medal Book published by special arrangement
with Field Newspaper Syndicate.

All inquiries should be addressed to Hall House, Inc.,
262 Mason Street, Greenwich, Connecticut.

ISBN 0-449-13964-6

Printed in the United States of America

10   9   8   7   6   5   4   3   2   1

10-17

10-22

WHAT DO YOU AN' 'IM EVER FIND TO CHAT ABOUT, MARY?

MUST BE VERY ENLIGHTENIN'

WINES AN' SPIRITS MOSTLY

VERY, FLO, 'E'S USUALLY FULL OF THE SUBJECT!

THEY CAME AN' TOOK EVERYTHIN' AWAY IN THEIR VAN —SOB— THEY'VE LEFT THE 'OUSE BARE EXCEPT F' THE CURTAINS!

I'LL GET MESELF DOWN TO THE OFFICE AN' CHECK UP—

THEY SAID THEY WERE FROM THE FINANCE COMPANY BUT I WAS TOO UPSET TO ASK FOR THEIR CREDENTIALS

WHO?

SKIP IT, THEY MIGHT SEND 'EM BACK F' THE CURTAINS!

10-29
Smythe

11-20   Smythe

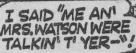

YOU SAID YOU WERE GOIN' SHOPPIN' — BUT I BET YOU'VE BEEN TO BINGO AGAIN!

12-2

GUESS 'OW MUCH I WON, PET

SORRY FOR KEEPIN' YOU IN THE DARK

SILLY GIRL! YOU DON'T 'AVE TO APOLOGISE

'E DOESN'T MIND WHERE 'E'S KEPT, SO LONG AS 'E'S KEPT!

Smythe

COULD FLORRIE BORROW YOUR ELECTRIC DRILL, ERIC? SHE WANTS TO PUT UP A COUPLE O' SHELVES IN THE KITCHEN

12-3

SURE, ANDY—

I'M AFRAID IT'LL NEED A NEW PLUG PUTTIN' ON IT

THAT'S ALL RIGHT, ERIC—I'LL POP BACK AFTER LUNCH

12-6

4-5

4-7

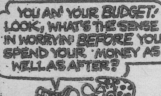

4-21

4.23

4·28

5-6

5-12

5-20

Smythe

6-7

Smythe

Follow the escapades of Andy Capp in these hilarious books by Smythe:

ANDY CAPP, MAN OF THE HOUR ·	13593-4	1.25
ANDY CAPP SOUNDS OFF	13805-4	1.25
ANDY CAPP STRIKES BACK (abridged)	13788-0	1.25
ANDY CAPP, THE ONE AND ONLY	13684-1	1.25
HARD AT WORK, ANDY CAPP?	13725-2	1.25
HATS OFF, ANDY CAPP	13769-4	1.25
HURRAY FOR ANDY CAPP (abridged)	P3550	1.25
IN YOUR EYE, ANDY CAPP (abridged)	13590-X	1.25
IT'S PUB TIME, ANDY CAPP	13609-4	1.25
KEEP 'EM ROLLING, ANDY CAPP	13841-0	1.25
LIVE IT UP, ANDY CAPP!	P3565	1.25
MEET ANDY CAPP	13716-3	1.25
NONE OF YOUR LIP, ANDY CAPP!	13719-8	1.25
NICE TO SEE YOU, ANDY CAPP	13848-8	1.25
RIGHT ON CUE, ANDY CAPP	13589-6	1.25
RISE & SHINE, ANDY CAPP	13708-2	1.25
TAKE A BOW, ANDY CAPP	13629-9	1.25
THE UNDISPUTED ANDY CAPP	13668-X	1.25
WATCH YOUR STEP, ANDY CAPP	P3562	1.25
WHAT NEXT, ANDY CAPP	13628-0	1.25
YOU'RE A RIOT, ANDY CAPP	13591-8	1.25
YOU'RE SOME HERO, ANDY CAPP	P3561	1.25
YOU'RE THE BOSS, ANDY CAPP	13631-0	1.25
YOU TELL 'EM ANDY CAPP	13594-2	1.25
VERY SNEAKY, ANDY CAPP	13627-2	1.25

FAWCETT BOOKS, P.O. Box 1014, Greenwich, Conn. 06830

Please send me the books I have checked above. Orders for less than 5 books must include 60¢ for the first book and 25¢ for each additional book to cover mailing and handling. Orders of 5 or more books postage is Free. I enclose $_____ in check or money order.

Name_____

Address_____

City_____ State/Zip_____

Please allow 4 to 5 weeks for delivery. This offer expires 6/78.